Jump Starts FOR CATECHISTS

BILL, PATTY, AND LISA COLEMAN

Key Teachings

TWENTY-THIRD PUBLICATIONS

185 WILLOW STREET • PO BOX 180 • MYSTIC, CT 06355
TEL: 1-800-321-0411 • FAX: 1-800-572-0788
Bayard   E-MAIL: ttpubs@aol.com • www.twentythirdpublications.com

Key Teachings

Twenty-Third Publications
A Division of Bayard
185 Willow Street
P.O. Box 180
Mystic, CT 06355
(860) 536-2611 or (800) 321-0411
www.twentythirdpublications.com
ISBN:1-58595-353-9

Contents

About This Series

The *Jump Starts for Catechists* series offers catechists
quick, hands-on tips for their faith formation sessions.
Each booklet provides practical and "classroom-tested"
information, formation, and ideas
that are valuable for beginning
as well as experienced catechists.
The books are written by some of
Twenty-Third Publications best-selling authors,
including Gwen Costello and Sr. Mary Kathleen Glavich.
Other books available in this series include
Seasonal Activities, and *Rites & Rituals*, and *Discipline Tips*

Key Teachings
This accessible and fact-filled Catholic resource
offers a wealth of information
• about Jesus and his message
• the Bible and the people and events in it
• the Mass, the sacraments, and their rituals
• the church, its beliefs, its saints, its prayers, and its traditions.
It's an ideal, at-your-fingertips reference book
for catechists.
Its simplicity and ease of use
also make it ideal for parents
whose children are preparing for the sacraments.

CHAPTER ONE

Jesus at the Center

The center of all Christianity
   is Jesus of Nazareth,
   the Christ, the Son of God.
For twenty centuries, his followers have thought about him,
   dreamed about him,
   talked about him,
   prayed to him,
   and then written about their insights in many forms.

Coming to know and love Jesus
   is more than an intellectual pursuit,
   more than amassing information.
It is a mystical and emotional experience as well,
   much like a boy who falls in love
     with the girl who lives next door.
For years he had known about her,
   the color of her hair, her height, her family background,
   her friends, her education, her job,
     even her likes and dislikes.

Yet, all of this was only knowledge,
the kind of information he had about many other friends.
Then, suddenly his eyes were opened
and he was able to go beyond
his knowing about her to love her,
a love which transformed his knowledge
and made it so profound
it turned his whole life upside down.
Our prayer is that your eyes will be opened
to see beyond your present knowledge of Jesus
to love him—
and perhaps to turn your life upside down.

The Sign of the Cross

*Because most people find the words of the Nicene Creed abstract
and hard to understand, another, simpler statement of faith in
Jesus' divinity was devised. We call it the Sign of the Cross.*

In this short creed
we profess our faith in three profound mysteries
which are the bedrock of all Christian belief:
the Trinity,
the divinity of Jesus,
and the saving power of his death on the cross.

In the name

(Notice this is singular, for there is only one God.)

of the Father, and of the Son, and of the Holy Spirit.

*(Notice the equality among the three names which tell us there are
three persons, for only persons have names.)*

Amen.

*(We affirm our belief in these profound mysteries by saying "Yes, so
be it," Amen.)*

We make the sign of the cross on our bodies to remember,
"He suffered under Pontius Pilate,
was crucified, died, and was buried.
On the third day he rose from the dead."

Why Jesus?

Why did God send Jesus? Jesus himself answered this question quite simply, "I came that they may have life, and have it abundantly." —John 10:10

For centuries, theologians and mystics
have meditated on these words,
trying to understand this abundant life that Jesus came to give.
From their writings we can distill four important truths
about the purpose of Jesus' life.

1. Because Jesus became our brother, "like us in all things except sin" (Hebrews 4:15), we can be a part of God's own family. We can experience a oneness with the Father as our brother, Jesus, did.

2. The presence of Jesus among us teaches us the intensity of God's love for all humanity.

3. By observing the lifestyle of Jesus, we learn how to live as God wants us to live.

4. Because Jesus became one of us, his love of the Father and of us, his human brothers and sisters, forged a bridge between us and God. When we accept Jesus and his commandments to love God and our neighbor, we are saved from lives of selfishness and sin.

Imitating Jesus

Abstract theological words, while filled with meaning, can so easily appear distant from our everyday lives. Here is a simple story of how one man discovered the meaning of the Incarnation.

Before integration,
>   black people in the southern United States lived in one world,
>   whites in another.

I was white, highly educated, and at least middle-class
>   but for some reason which still is not clear to me,
>   I wanted to become friends with poor, uneducated, black people
>   and somehow become a part of their community.

I joined the NAACP
>   and began attending their meetings
>   which were held in
>   a little ramshackle church each week.

One afternoon, the president invited me
>   to give the opening prayer.

As I prayed, I heard voices shouting
>   from every corner of the church,
>   "Amen," "Yes," "All right," "You tell 'em, brother."

In that moment, I knew I was accepted.

I had become one of the community.
>   I was still white and they were black.
>   I was still educated and most of them were not.
>   I was still middle-class while they were poor.

Yet, I was one of them.
>   They called me "brother" and really meant it.

As I left the meeting
>   I remembered the old catechism word:
>   Incarnation.

Without ceasing to be the all-wise and all-wonderful God,
>   Jesus became our humble human brother.

And yes, it seemed to me
>   that we who follow Jesus must do as he did,
>   become a part of the persecuted, poor
>   and forgotten human community.

For me, that is what Incarnation means.

The Kingdom of God

Jesus inherited many expressions from the Jewish culture in which he lived and made them his own. No expression is more common and perhaps more misunderstood than this one.

Gospel writers remembered
    that Jesus told his hearers to change their hearts
    for the kingdom of God was at hand.
Jesus cured the sick, cast out demons,
    forgave sins, and announced the good news
    that the kingdom of God was breaking in
        on human history.
His cures, his power over demons, his preaching were signs,
    signs that even the simplest could understand
    that indeed the kingdom of God was at hand.
Jesus insisted this kingdom which—
    like a mustard seed or leaven in the dough—
    will grow slowly, imperceptibly perhaps.

For individuals, only heaven will bring
    the kind of justice and contentment
        promised by God.
For society, however,
    the kingdom will continue to grow
    and quietly destroy evils
        until Jesus returns in glory at the end of this era.
All of this was in Jesus' mind
    when he taught us to pray,
    "Thy kingdom come."
Then, to be sure everyone understood
    just what the kingdom entailed,
    he added,
        "Thy will be done on earth as it is in heaven."

Theological Words about Jesus

Through the centuries theologians have invented words to express the mystery of Jesus. Many of them come from the fourth century when the whole church struggled to define its belief in the divinity of Jesus. Others are from the time of the Reformation when Catholic theologians tried to express their faith in clearer and more concise ways. Here are some of the technical, theological words Christians use to discuss the mystery of Jesus.

Consubstantial

Jesus is God just as the Father is God. They posess the same divine nature. It is not enough to say that he was the finest human who ever lived or even that he had a special relationship with God. Christians believe that Jesus is God.

Hypostatic union

Once we believe that Jesus is God we must not forget that he is at the same time fully human, with all that entails.

Nicene Creed

A formula of belief named from the First Ecumenical Council held in Nicaea in 325 A.D. It is the creed Catholics say at Sunday Mass and puts great emphasis on the divinity of Jesus.

Incarnation

The act by which God united himself to a human nature. This happened when the angel announced to Mary that she would be the mother of the Savior.

The Apostles Creed

An ancient baptismal creed with roots in the first century AD. Catholics say it any time they renew their baptismal promises.

Substance

A philosophical word meaning the essence of a thing and answers the question, what is it? All three Persons in God have one substance for there is only one God.

Person

A philosophical word which names an intelligent substance and answers the question, who is it? In the one God (one substance) there are three distinct Persons: Father, Son, and Holy Spirit. Jesus is the Second Person, the Son.

Trinity

A philosophical word used by Christians for the three Persons in the one God.

Virgin birth

God the Father was the father of Jesus. Mary, his mother, remained a virgin before and after the birth of Jesus.

Christology

Theological study of Jesus, the Christ who lives in the church through the Holy Spirit.

Titles of Jesus

Early Christians used many different words to describe Jesus. Some of them throw light on what they believed him to be, fully human and yet fully divine.

Jesus of Nazareth

He came to us in human form, "born of a woman" as St. Paul says, with clear historical origins and a connection with one town and one people.

Son of Mary

From the beginning Christians treasured the memory of his mother, Mary, and insisted that she had a prominent role in her son's saving work.

The Messiah, "the anointed one"

People were anointed to perform a special task such as to be a king or prophet or priest. Jews looked forward to one who was anointed by God to initiate his kingdom on earth.

Son of Man

In the Book of Daniel a figure appears called the Son of Man. The title was mystical and mysterious. Because early believers recognized in Jesus something beyond their understanding, this title seemed apt.

Son of God

From the beginning, Christians believed that Jesus was God's own Son. They did not know how to express this overpowering reality since they believed in only one God and so used this title Son to come as close as they dared to an incredible reality of faith.

The Lord

This is one of the Jewish words used for God. Early believers said quite openly, "Jesus is Lord."

The Suffering Servant

The Prophet Isaiah called the nation of Israel the servant of the Lord, a servant called to suffer. Early believers saw that Jesus was a summation of all that was best in Israel and so suffered as the servant of his Father.

The Good Shepherd

A traditional title in the Hebrew Scriptures for God who shepherds his people, Israel. Jesus applied it to himself to emphasize his intimate knowledge and care for his followers.

Devotions to Jesus

Through the centuries since Jesus' death and resurrection, saints and mystics have imagined him in many different ways, ways that made it easier for them to pray.

Here are a few of the ways Christians of our past have thought about and prayed to Jesus.

Christ the King

Jesus is pictured as ruler of the universe who leads the way to God's kingdom. He taught through word and example that service to others is the way to this kingdom.

The Sacred Heart

Pictures of Jesus show his wounded heart exposed with a crown of thorns entwined about it. This devotion stresses the compassion and love Jesus has for all humankind and the suffering that love caused him.

The Precious Blood

Among ancient people, blood was a symbol of life. Death came when the blood was poured out. This devotion calls attention to the price Jesus paid for his compassion toward humanity.

The Holy Name of Jesus

The name of a person answers the question, who are you. Devotion to the name of Jesus is to his unique personality which united both the human and divine.

The Eucharistic Jesus

Catholics believe that Jesus is present in the appearances of bread and wine in the Eucharist. This devotion encourages frequent reception of Holy Communion and prayer before the Blessed Sacrament.

Jesus, the Prophet

Jesus can easily be pictured as the Father's spokesperson, the one who brings his message to the world. This devotion stresses the determined courage of Jesus in the face of powerful opposition.

The Priestly Jesus

Jesus is sometimes pictured in priestly robes offering himself as a sacrifice. He is both the priest who offers the sacrifice and the victim.

Gospel Parables

A parable is a story whose meaning is not immediately obvious.
Parables take a little pondering
   to get into the meat of their meaning.
Jesus, like many Oriental sages,
   loved the parable.
It allowed him to talk about a profound truth
   in words that did not frighten simple people.
At their own speed and in their own way,
   they would probe the story and, when ready,
   uncover its meaning.
A parable might sit on the edge of one's mind for years
   before being understood.
On the other hand, someone else might understand it
   almost immediately.
Here are some of Jesus' most remembered parables,
   where you can find them in the gospels,
   and a hint of what they may mean to you.

The Salt of the Earth (Matthew 5:13)

Jesus' followers add an invisible yet essential ingredient to human history.

The Light of the World (Matthew 5:14–16)

We who follow Jesus are overcoming the world's evil.

The Sower (Matthew 13:4–9)

Not everyone who hears Jesus' message does something about it.

The Wheat and the Weeds (Matthew 13:24–30)

Good and evil will exist side by side, often appearing much alike.

The Mustard Seed (Matthew 13:31–32)

Goodness will overcome evil.

The Net (Matthew 13:47–50)

God's justice will win out.

The Lost Sheep (Matthew 18:12–14)
God cares about sinners. No one is outside God's love.

The Unforgiving Debtor (Matthew 18:23–35)
God cannot forgive us if we do not forgive one another.

The Vineyard Laborers (Matthew 20:1–16)
God's ways are very different from ours.

The Two Sons (Matthew 21:28–32)
No sinner is so evil God does not love him or her.

The Wicked Farmers (Matthew 21:33–46)
Those who reject God's love will be punished.

The Wedding Feast (Matthew 22:1–14)
We will meet the most unlikely people in heaven.

The Ten Bridesmaids (Matthew 25:1–13)
We must be alert to the opportunities God gives us.

The Talents (Matthew 25:14–30)
To whom much has been given much will be expected.

The Sheep and the Goats (Matthew 25:31–46)
We serve God best by caring for our neighbors.

The Good Samaritan (Luke 10:29–37)
Life's outcasts are often God's closest friends.

The Insistent Friend (Luke 11:5–8)
God does hear our prayers.

The Prodigal Son (Luke 15:11–32)
God is always waiting for us to repent.

The Pharisee and the Publican (Luke 18:9–14)
Humility is a cornerstone of holiness.

CHAPTER TWO

The Bible

Any search for Jesus takes us to the Bible, to the writings that helped form his childhood faith. The Bible consists of the Old Testament, also called the Hebrew Scriptures, and the New Testament, also called the Christian Scriptures.

The word Bible comes from the Greek word,
    biblios, for book.
It is the official collection of writings
    that believers accept as the authentic word of God.

Over the centuries first the Jewish community
    and later the Christian church
    decided which ancient writings
    were to be included in the Bible.
The Bible is not only the word of God
    but the work of the communities of faith as well.
Christians and Jews are sometimes called
    "people of the Book."
We reverence this holy collection
    and believe that God inspired its authors.

Jews and Christians alike base their religious beliefs
  on their sacred Scriptures.
Few of us are able to read the ancient languages
  in which these books were originally written
  or know much about the subtleties
    of their cultural and historical context
  that so influence their meaning.
Our best guide in understanding the Bible
  is the living church
    with all its resources
    and its centuries of experience.

The Old Testament

Following Jesus inevitably creates in us a desire to understand the religious culture in which he lived. Because the Jewish people preserved their heritage, we know a great deal about what happened to the Jewish people in the time before Jesus. We find this information in that collection of the 46 ancient writings of the Old Testament.

The Pentateuch

The first five books of the Bible
  are called the Pentateuch (which means five).
They explore human origins,
    God's choice of the Hebrew people,
    the covenant or treaty God made with them,
    and the Law that was Israel's obligation
      under the covenant.
Originally oral traditions,
    these books were written and rewritten
      over hundreds of years.
They define Hebrew identity
    and are the foundation of all Hebrew life.

The books of the Pentateuch are:

1. The Book of Genesis: stories that lead to God's choice of Israel as his special people.

2. The Book of Exodus: stories of God's deliverance of Israel and his covenant with them.

3. The Book of Leviticus: rules and regulations for living in the covenant.

4. The Book of Numbers: more rules, regulations, and the stories behind them.

5. The Book of Deuteronomy: stories of Israel's entry into the Promised Land.

The Historical Books

These sixteen books
  recount many of the high points of Hebrew history
    from the entry into Palestine
    to within a century of Jesus' coming.
Ancient peoples did not write history as we do.
They told stories, recorded sermons,
  and tried to explain why things happened as they did.
The historical books include:

1. Joshua
2. Judges
3. Ruth
4. First Samuel
5. Second Samuel
6. First Kings
7. Second Kings
8. First Chronicles
9. Second Chronicles
10. Ezra
11. Nehemiah
12. Tobit
13. Judith
14. Esther
15. First Maccabees
16. Second Maccabees

The Wisdom Books

These are seven books
of poems, prayers, practical advice, and wise sayings.
The Wisdom books include:

1. Job
2. Psalms
3. Proverbs
4. Ecclesiastes
5. Song of Songs, also called
Song of Solomon

6. Wisdom, also called
Wisdom of Solomon
7. Sirach, also called
Ecclesiasticus

The Prophets

These eighteen books contain
the poems, pronouncements, and stories of the prophets,
people called by God to deliver his message to Israel.
Prophets had no official standing in Israel.
They had only their lives and their message
to recommend them.
Jesus and John the Baptist were considered prophets
by many of their contemporaries.
The prophetic books include:

1. Isaiah
2. Jeremiah
3. Lamentations
4. Baruch
5. Ezekiel
6. Daniel
7. Hosea
8. Joel
9. Amos

10. Obadiah
11. Jonah
12. Micah
13. Nahum
14. Habakkuk
15. Zephaniah
16. Haggai
17. Zechariah
18. Malachi

The New Testament

Anyone searching for Jesus
  will turn to the Christian Scriptures or the "New Testament."
It is a collection of twenty-seven documents
  written by early disciples of Jesus
  probably during the second half of the first century.
The word "testament" means a treaty or covenant agreement
  between God and all who believe in Jesus,
    just as the "Old Testament"
    is a covenant between God and the Israelites.
Scholars don't always know
  exactly when each book was written
  or who the authors were,
    even though tradition assigns a specific disciple
    as the author of each book.

The Gospels

These are four collections of the sayings and actions of Jesus, woven together around the main events of his life. They include:

1. The gospel according to Matthew, written between 70–75 AD.

2. The gospel according to Mark, written between 65–70 AD.

3. The gospel according to Luke, written between 70–80 AD.

4. The gospel according to John, written between 90–99 AD.

The Acts of the Apostles

This is an intriguing view of the first disciples and the early journeys of St. Paul written by St. Luke, probably about the same time as his version of the gospel (70–80 AD).

The Letters of St. Paul

These are letters written by St. Paul (or traditionally attributed to Paul) to different communities of faith and to other Christian missionaries.

1. To the church in Rome, written about 58 AD.

2. First letter to the church in Corinth, written about 56 AD.

3. Second letter to the church in Corinth, written about 57 AD.

4. To the church in Galatia, written about 54–55 AD.

5. To the church in Ephesus, written about 62 (or 80-100) AD.

6. To the church in Philippi, written about 56 AD.

7. To the church in Colossae, written about 62 AD.

8. First letter to the church in Thessalonica, written about 51 AD.

9. Second letter to Thessalonica, written about 51 (or 80–100) AD.

10. First letter to his coworker Timothy, written about 63–67 AD.

11. Second letter to his coworker Timothy, written about 63–67 AD.

12. To his coworker Titus, written about 63–67 AD.

13. To a fellow believer, Philemon, written about 62 AD.

14. To Hebrew Christians, date written uncertain, sometime between about 67 and 100 AD.

Letters to all Christians

These are letters by early church leaders that probably were written to be circulated to several churches.

1. The letter of St. James, written shortly before 62 AD.

2. First letter of St. Peter, written shortly before 62 AD.

3. Second letter of St. Peter, written at the end of the first century.

4. First letter of St. John, written about 90 AD.

5. Second letter of St. John, written about 90 AD.

6. Third letter of St. John, written about 90 AD.

7. The letter of St. Jude, written between 65 and 70 AD.

The Book of Revelation

This final book of the Bible was written in sometimes obscure symbolic language to encourage those early Christians who were undergoing persecution. It was probably written toward the end of the first century.

Bible Heroes and Heroines

All of the following people were part of Jesus' religious heritage.

Abraham

The first in a long line of historical figures with whom God made a covenant.

Isaac

The son of Abraham and Sarah, a man who kept alive the promise made to his father by God.

Jacob

A twin son of Isaac and Rebecca. He tricked his twin brother, Esau, and inherited the promise. He labored for years to obtain the hand of Rachel in marriage, and he fathered the twelve patriarchs who gave their names to the tribes of Israel or Jacob.

Joseph

One of Jacob's sons who was sold into slavery by his brothers, but who eventually saved his family from famine by bringing them to Egypt.

Moses

With his brother, Aaron, he challenged Egyptian power and led the Hebrews out of Egypt into the desert. He gave the Hebrews the laws he received from God and organized the nation.

Joshua

He led the Israelites out of the desert and into Palestine, where they conquered the native Canaanites.

The Judges

These were early rulers of the Israelites in Palestine. At that time the tribes had no clear central organization and they relied on the Judges to lead them.

Samson

The most popular of all the Judges who fought against the newly arrived Philistines.

Ruth

A woman who provides a link between the days of the Judges and the monarchy of the Israelites.

Samuel

The last of the Judges and a prophet who witnessed the transition to the monarchy, which he opposed.

Saul

Anointed by Samuel as the first king of Israel, he was later rejected and died in battle.

David

The heroic second king of Israel. As a boy he killed the Philistine giant Goliath. Later he was outlawed by Saul. Upon Saul's death, he became king of Israel and extended its boundaries in all directions. Many of the biblical psalms are attributed to David.

Solomon

He was David's son who became Israel's king and a man known to have an "understanding heart." Later in life, he turned away from the Lord. Upon his death, his kingdom was divided into two competing monarchies, one headquartered in Jerusalem and the other in Samaria.

Elijah

The first of a long line of men and women we call prophets who delivered messages from the Lord and called on Israel to put its faith into practice. Elijah opposed the kings of Samaria, then a part of Israel, and their injustice and worship of false gods.

Elisha

The successor of Elijah, he was a man of miracles and outspoken opposition to false worship and injustice.

Amos

He was a humble farmer called by God to speak against the luxury and injustice of the people in the Samarian court.

Hosea

A prophet who had a faithless wife, Hosea wrote of Israel as the faithless bride of God.

Jeremiah

He was a man called by God to guide Jerusalem through the final days before its destruction by the Babylonians. He was hated by Jerusalem's ruling class and probably died in Egyptian exile.

Isaiah

A prophet who lived just before and during the Babylonian exile, Isaiah's poetry is filled with hope.

Daniel

This is a mythical character whose name is given to one of the biblical books that encouraged Jews during one of their most terrifying persecutions.

Job

Because he struggled with the problem of why bad things happen to good people, Job is an example of faith and trust.

Esther

She was a great popular heroine of the Jews during their persecutions.

Judith

Another popular heroine, Judith led the Jews to victory over their enemies.

The Maccabees

They were a Jewish family who led a resistance movement against the pagan rulers who attempted to obliterate their religion and culture in the second century B.C.

Gospel People

In this alphabetical list are some of the people you will meet as you read the four gospels:

Anna

An old woman who recognized Jesus as the messiah while he was still an infant.

Annas

The father-in-law of the high priest Caiaphas and a powerful Jewish leader.

Apostles

The twelve men Jesus chose to be his closest followers: Simon Peter, Andrew, James the greater, John, Philip, Bartholomew (also called Nathanael), Thomas, Matthew (also called Levi), James the less, Thaddaeus (also called Jude), Simon the Zealot, and Judas who betrayed Jesus.

Barabbas

A revolutionary held prisoner by the Romans and who was released by Pilate in place of Jesus.

Caiaphas

The Jewish high priest who first suggested that Jesus be executed.

Cleopas

A disciple who met Jesus on the road to Emmaus.

Elizabeth

Mother of John the Baptist and a cousin of Mary.

Gabriel

The angel who told Mary she was to be the mother of the messiah.

Herod

King of Judea at the time of Jesus' birth, who ordered the slaughter of the innocent children of Bethlehem.

James

An apostle called by Jesus with his brother John while both were fishing. Also the name of another apostle who was the son of Alphaeus, sometimes called James the less. A third James was the leader of the early church in Jerusalem.

John
The apostle, brother of James, believed to be the author of the fourth gospel and some of the epistles.

John the Baptist
A cousin of Jesus and the man who prepared the Jewish people for his coming.

Joseph
The husband of Mary and foster-father of Jesus.

Joseph of Arimathea
Follower of Jesus in whose tomb Jesus' body was laid.

Judas
The apostle who betrayed Jesus.

Lazarus
A friend whom Jesus raised from the dead, brother of Martha and Mary.

Luke
Author of the third gospel, probably a companion of St. Paul.

Mark
Author of the second gospel and probably an early disciple of Jesus, although not one of the Twelve.

Martha
Sister of Mary and Lazarus and a friend of Jesus.

Mary
The mother of Jesus.

Mary Magdalene
A early follower of Jesus who was one of the first to see the risen Christ.

Mary, sister of Martha and Lazarus
A friend of Jesus.

Matthew

A tax collector turned apostle who wrote the first gospel. He is also called Levi.

Nicodemus

A leader of the Jewish people who came to visit Jesus at night so he would not be seen with him by others.

Peter

Peter or rock is the name Jesus gave to Simon, the most outspoken of the apostles and their natural leader, to remind him that he was to be the rock upon which Jesus would build his church.

Pharisees

A Jewish sect or party which insisted on a rigorous observance of the Law. These men were very hostile toward Jesus.

Pontius Pilate

Roman governor of Palestine who, at the request of the Jewish leaders, ordered Jesus' death.

Sadducees

A political party within the Judaism of Jesus' time, concentrated among the priests and Temple leaders.

Scribes

The learned Jewish people of Jesus' day who were called "Rabbi".

Simeon

A Temple prophet who recognized Jesus' special role, even while Jesus was only an infant.

Simon of Cyrene

Man forced to carry Jesus' cross to Calvary.

Zacchaeus

A tax collector who climbed into a tree to see Jesus and later changed his life to follow him.

Zechariah

Father of John the Baptist.

CHAPTER THREE

The Church

Church Organization

We follow Jesus not alone
    but in community.
Our community, the Roman Catholic church,
    is both ancient and modern.
Understanding all its organizational subtleties
    can be a challenge.

The Catholic church
    is an organized community of faith.
With twenty centuries of history behind it
    and scores of reforms and renewals in its past,
    the church has evolved into a very complicated
    and perhaps confusing structure.
In spite of its complexity,
    church organization works well
    and provides most church members
      with a maximum of freedom
      and strong support in time of need.

The International Church

The pope

Chief administrator and teacher of the world church, bishop of the diocese of Rome, patriarch of the Latin Rite, head of the college of bishops, and ruler of the tiny independent country, the Vatican State

Curia

Officials who help the pope in his work of teaching, governing, and administering. The Secretariat of State, for example, maintains diplomatic relations with many countries and often negotiates with heads of state concerning the religious rights of their own citizens. There are also congregations for such works as: worship, canonization of saints, the clergy, religious, education, and evangelization. Other offices are called secretariats, tribunals, commissions, and institutes. They deal with a variety of concerns from promoting Christian unity to disputes between dioceses, from matters of justice and peace to financial administration. All are responsible to the pope.

College of cardinals

A group of men, appointed to a life term by the pope, who meet to elect the next pope and occasionally to give the pope advice on important matters. Individual cardinals hold many diverse offices in the church. Some work in the Roman curia while others are heads of important dioceses throughout the world. Centuries ago, the cardinals were the bishops near Rome, the pastors of certain Roman churches, and deacons in Rome. This tradition is still maintained by calling some cardinal bishops, others cardinal priests, and others cardinal deacons.

The synod of bishops

Bishops around the world elect representatives and send them to Rome every third year to dialogue with the pope on important matters such as Christian marriage, the need for vocations, the role of women.

Ecumenical council

A meeting of all the bishops of the world held to clarify matters of belief or to give direction to church policy. There have been only twenty such councils in the history of the church. The most recent was Vatican II held in the 1960s.

Religious communities

Men and/or women who have joined together to live lives dedicated to Jesus and the church through public vows of poverty, chastity, and obedience. These religious orders or communities often serve in many different countries and some maintain a worldwide office in Rome.

The Regional Church

National conferences of bishops

The bishops in individual countries (or groups of countries when they are very small) meet regularly to coordinate policy on matters that affect all their members. They elect a president, usually have a permanent staff to carry out their policies, and elect representatives to the world synod held every third year in Rome. The pope keeps in contact with the bishops of a country through a representative usually called the "apostolic delegate."

The Diocesan Church

The bishop

The shepherd of all who live in his diocese is called the "ordinary" of that diocese. He may be assisted by other "auxiliary bishops." If it has been agreed that one of these auxiliary bishops will succeed the ordinary when he dies or retires, this person is called a "coadjutor." The bishop is also associated with one church in his diocese, which is called the cathedral.

The chancery

A group of priests, deacons, sisters, brothers, and laypeople who help the bishop in his work. The bishop's first assistant is called a "vicar general." Others may help with finances and management (the chancellor), education, charity, priests' assignments, marriage preparation, liturgy, evangelization, etc. Their task is to provide research and specialized services for the parishes of the diocese.

The Parish Church

The pastor

The chief administrator and teacher of the local church. He may be helped by other priests called "parochial vicars" and/or by a variety of others: deacons, pastoral assistants, ministers to the sick, directors of religious education, ministers of music, social service coordinators, etc.

The parish council

Most parishes today have an advisory group selected from the parish to assist the pastor and other parish employees.

Parish societies

Most societies are directly responsible to the pastor. One notable exception is the Knights of Columbus. They work closely with their pastors but are not a part of the church's official organization.

More About the Parish

A parish is a community of believers headed by a priest called the pastor. It is here that most people find the support and help they need in their following of Jesus. Parishes provide many helps to those seeking a deeper and richer spiritual life.

Worship

Every Sunday and most weekdays members of the community celebrate the Lord's Supper together. These gatherings are commonly called "the Liturgy" or "the Mass." Everyone is welcome.

Special sacraments

Sacraments mark watershed times in the lives of believers and are celebrated in the parish, often during the Sunday liturgy.

Care of the sick

Holy Communion, Bible readings, and prayers provide worship opportunities in hospitals, nursing homes, and residences for those too ill or infirm to celebrate with the whole community of parishioners are an important part of parish life. They include novenas in honor of Jesus, Mary or favorite saints, prayer groups, the rosary, the way of the cross, retreats, missions, and other prayer opportunities Catholics treasure.

Counseling

Most parishes provide special programs for people about to be married, for couples who are searching for ways to enrich their marriages, for individuals who are trying to reform their lives, and to many who are troubled. The sacrament of penance (also called confession and reconciliation) provides an opportunity for people to talk over their goals and progress toward them with a priest.

Devotions

Prayer services with appeal to special groups of parishioners are an important part of parish life. They include novenas in honor of Jesus, Mary, or favorite saints, prayer groups, the rosary, the way of the cross, retreats, missions, and other prayer opportunities Catholics treasure.

Education

There are a wide variety of educational opportunities open to parishioners of most parishes. Some provide Catholic schools for youth. Most have special religious education programs for children, youth ministry opportunities for teens, and special adult offerings for older parishioners as well as parish-wide efforts during Lent, Advent, and at other special times during the year.

Service

Most parishes have service groups like the St. Vincent de Paul Society or the Legion of Mary, and encourage all parishioners to participate in supporting a variety of worthy causes. More and more parishes combine local service with a study of the underlying causes of social problems like poverty, violence, hopelessness, racial conflicts, disintegration of families, etc. As a result, many Catholics become politically active in reform movements.

Community-building

Church suppers, parties, parent-teen programs and a variety of other activities help promote a deepening of parish community. In addition, many parish societies have a strong social dimension with regular meetings and many fund-raising activities.

Leadership

Parishioners may work with their parish staff by serving as officers of various parish societies, on the parish council and other governing boards, as lectors and eucharistic ministers at Mass, as ministers to the sick, as liturgy planners, in the parish music program, and in many other leadership roles.

Growth

One of the parish's most important tasks is to deepen its own awareness of the impact of the gospel on current topics like war and peace, nuclear arms, human rights, world hunger, abortion, pornography, and the use of money. Homilies, special programs, discussions, and distribution of literature all help in this kind of growth. While different parishioners may hold different opinions on these topics, all are expected to respect the opinions of others and to try to learn from interacting with them.

Catholic Heroes and Heroines

Christians have always treasured the memory of men and women whose lives were an inspiration to the whole community. Here is a list of some of the more popular saints and the ages in which they lived.

The First Century, age of our Christian beginnings

St. Peter, the leader of the apostles, martyred in Rome

St. Paul, apostle to the Gentiles, also martyred in Rome

St. Mary Magdalene, friend of Jesus

St. Clement, pope and defender of church unity

The Second Century, an era of growth

St. Ignatius, bishop of Antioch, writer, martyr

St. Polycarp, bishop, martyr, disciple of St. John

The Third Century, an era of intense persecution

St. Cecilia, martyr and patroness of church music

St. Lawrence, deacon, friend of the poor

The Fourth Century, Christianity becomes official

St. Anthony, founder of Egyptian monastic life

St. Martin of Tours, apostle to France

St. Augustine, North African theologian and bishop

St. Nicholas, whom we honor today as Santa Claus

St. Agnes, teenage martyr of Rome

St. Jerome, biblical scholar and hermit

St. Ambrose, theologian and bishop

St. Monica, mystic and mother of St. Augustine

The Fifth Century, invasion of Europe by barbarian tribes

St. John Chrysostom, defender of the Trinity

St. Patrick, apostle to Ireland

St. Brigid of Ireland, founder of monasteries for men and for women

St. Genevieve, protector of Paris from Hun invaders

St. Hilary, popular saint who was once excommunicated

The Sixth Century, an era of new beginnings

St. Benedict, founder of monastic life in Europe

St. Scholastica, sister of Benedict and herself a religious leader

The Seventh Century, a time of conflict

St. Cuthbert, English missionary bishop

St. Oswald, king of Scotland

The Eighth Century, an era of reform and confusion

St. John Damascene, teacher, writer, and mystic

St. Boniface, apostle to the German peoples

The Ninth Century, Europe's attempt to reorganize

St. Ansgar, apostle to Scandinavia

Saints Cyril and Methodius, apostles to the Slavic peoples

The Tenth Century, Europe's darkest age

St. Olga, grandduchess of Kiev and mother of Russian Christianity

St. Stephen, apostle to Hungary

The Eleventh Century, end of the dark ages

St. Anselm, teacher, theologian, and counselor

St. Ladislaus, king of Poland and early advocate of religious liberty

St. Peter Damian, monk and church reformer who became a cardinal only when threatened with excommunication if he refused to honor the appointment.

The Twelfth Century, beginning of a new era

St. Bernard of Clairvaux, reformer, writer, advocate of devotion to Mary

St. Thomas Becket, English archbishop martyred in his own cathedral

St. Hildegard, called wisest woman of her age

The Thirteenth Century, an age of scholars and saints

St. Francis of Assisi, poet, mystic, friend of the poor

St. Dominic, mystic, preacher, and reformer

St. Clare, founder of the Poor Clares

St. Anthony of Padua, teacher and preacher

St. Albert the Great, teacher and scientific pioneer

St. Thomas Aquinas, considered by many the greatest theologian in Christian history

St. Bonaventure, mystic and theologian

The Fourteenth Century, beginning of a decline

St. Brigid, Swedish queen and reformer

St. Catherine of Siena, counselor to popes, mystic

The Fifteenth Century, an era of decline

St. Catherine of Genoa, widow and renowned teacher

St. Joan of Arc, French military leader burned at the stake

The Sixteenth Century, Christianity divided in Europe

St. Thomas More, chancellor of England and martyr

St. John Fisher, bishop martyred in the Reformation conflict

St. Teresa of Avila, Spanish mystic and reformer

St. Ignatius of Loyola, founder of the Jesuits

St. John of the Cross, mystic and reformer

The Seventeenth Century, time of secularization in Europe

St. Vincent de Paul, organizer of charities

St. Francis de Sales, writer and spiritual guide

St. Peter Claver, apostle to slaves being brought to the Americas

St. Margaret Mary Alacoque, apostle of devotion to the Sacred Heart

St. Isaac Jogues, martyr and apostle to native Americans

St. Martin de Porres, heroic worker among slaves and outcasts in Peru

The Eighteenth Century, the era of petty persecution in Europe

St. Benedict Joseph Labre, pilgrim and mystic

St. Paul of the Cross, mystic and leader of church reform

St. Alphonsus Ligouri, apostle to the forgotten Italian poor

The Nineteenth Century, beginnings of a Catholic revival

St. John Bosco, apostle to the poor

St. Elizabeth Seton, American widow and founder of Catholic schools

St. John Vianney, French pastor and mystic

St. Bernadette, visionary and mystic

St. Thérèse of Lisieux, mystic and popular writer

St. John Neumann, American bishop

Bl. Damien of Molokai, apostle to the lepers

The Twentieth Century, a time of flowering

St. Pius X, pope and reformer

Venerable Matt Talbot, former alcoholic and Irish mystic

Bl. Charles de Foucauld, former soldier of fortune and hermit

Bl. John XXIII, pope, father of Vatican II and most loved Catholic leader of our era

St. Katharine Drexel, apostle to American Blacks and Indians

St. Maximilian Kolbe, priest and martyr in a Nazi concentration camp

Bl. Mother Teresa of Calcutta, apostle to the poor of India

Dorothy Day, apostle of peace and service to the poor

St. Frances Cabrini, American citizen, worker among Italian immigrants

Oscar Romero, archbishop of San Salvador, martyred while celebrating Mass

The missionaries of El Salvador, North American women martyred for helping the poor

Our Catholic Tradition

Did you know that…

- kneeling is a sign of our humility before God? (Kneeling on one knee is called "genuflection.")
- standing is a sign of alertness and readiness to listen?
- the sign of the cross demonstrates belief in the Trinity and the power of Jesus' death to save us?
- using holy water is a reminder of our baptism?
- a prayer repeated once a day for nine consecutive days is called a novena?
- fasting and abstinence are forms of prayer? (Fasting means eating only one full meal on a given day and just enough at two other meals to maintain strength; abstinence means refraining from eating meat.)
- many American Catholics abstain every Friday as a prayer for world peace?
- fasting is practiced by most of the world's great religions?
- holding out one's hands palms upward is a sign of our dependence on God?
- Christians once turned toward Jerusalem when they prayed?
- the rosary is an excellent form of prayer for those who feel deep anxiety? (All the words said during the rosary come from either the Bible or very ancient traditions.)
- sitting or kneeling quietly before the Blessed Sacrament is a prayer? (Some Catholics spend all night in prayer before the Blessed Sacrament.)
- We honor Jesus present in the Eucharist with a devotion called benediction? (In benediction the consecrated host is placed in a holder called a "monstrance" so that all can see, and the priest blesses the assembly with the monstrance.)
- incense is sometimes burned at liturgies and devotions to

help people focus on their prayer? (Incense is a symbol of God's blessing enveloping the world.)

About the Church

Did you know that…

- there are over 1 billion Catholics in the world?
- over 60 million Americans are Catholic?
- Catholics live in every nation in the world, even in places where they are routinely persecuted?
- there are 200 archdioceses and dioceses in the United States?
- there are over 19,000 parishes in the United States?
- there have been 264 popes, beginning with St. Peter?
- there have been 37 anti-popes, men who claimed to be the pope but were rejected by the Church?
- for the first three centuries Christians were routinely persecuted by Roman officials?
- the Roman Emperor Constantine established Christianity as the religion of the Empire in 313 AD?
- an ecumenical council is a meeting of all the world's bishops?
- the first ecumenical council took place in 325 AD at a small town in present day Turkey called Nicaea?
- it took centuries and six ecumenical councils for Christians to work out a formula that expressed their belief in the Trinity?
- in 1054 the churches of the East (Orthodox) separated from those whose center of unity was in the pope of Rome (Catholic)?
- one medieval European heresy, Albigensianism, forbade their members to marry?
- the church established the early European universities? (Philosophy and theology were the only reputable sciences in the Middle Ages.)

- in the early 1400s, three men claimed to be the legitimate pope? All had cardinals and bishops among their supporters.
- the ordained church leadership is called the hierarchy?
- a belief stated in words is called a doctrine?
- Martin Luther, leader of the Protestant Reformation, in the sixteenth century, did not set out to divide the church but to reform it from within?
- John Calvin, another leader of Protestantism, ruled Geneva as its religious and temporal lord?
- Henry VIII of England was once given the title "Defender of the Faith" by the pope and later excommunicated?
- the ecumenical council held in Trent, Italy attempted to reform the church in response to the Protestant Reformation?
- American Catholicism began with Spanish settlers in Florida and Georgia?
- the first English Catholics settled in Maryland?
- the first Catholic bishop in the United States was John Carroll whose cousin signed the Declaration of Independence?
- parochial schools are an American invention?
- many American Catholic churches and convents were burned to the ground by rioting mobs in the nineteenth century?
- John Kennedy was the first Catholic to ever be elected president of the United States?
- Pope John XXIII hoped to reform the church and promote Christian unity by calling together the Second Vatican Council (Vatican II)?
- Vatican II was the twentieth ecumenical council?
- the American bishops have written forward-looking pastoral letters on peace, the economy, and other major issues?
- in Latin America the official church has made a "preferential option for the poor"?

CHAPTER FOUR

The Seven Sacraments

Those who follow Jesus believe they are never alone. Jesus, his Father, the Spirit, and the community of faith are ever with those who believe. There are seven sacred signs of God's presence in the lives of believers which we call sacraments.

Sacraments of Christian Initiation
These three sacraments immerse a person in the church, the Body of Christ:
  baptism
  confirmation
  eucharist

Sacraments of Healing
These two sacraments offer Christ's healing touch of forgiveness and peace:
  penance (reconciliation)
  anointing of the sick

Sacraments of Mission

These sacraments are expressions of the call of every baptized Christian to follow Christ in a particular way:

holy orders

matrimony

About the Sacraments

Did you know that…

• the Council of Trent (1543–1563) defined the traditional Christian belief in seven sacraments?

• all sacraments involve the whole community?

• the church itself is sometimes called the "eighth sacrament"?

• baptism welcomes a person into the Christian community?

• baptism is necessary to receive any other sacrament?

• baptism can be given in three ways: by immersing the whole body in water, by pouring water over the head, or by sprinkling water on the head?

• some theologians taught that unbaptized infants did not go to heaven but to a special place they called limbo? (Limbo is a theological opinion, not official church doctrine.)

• Catholics do not ordinarily rebaptize converts from other Christian denominations?

• in Eastern churches and among many Spanish-speaking peoples, confirmation is administered at baptism?

• in some Christian churches, confirmation must be administered before eucharist is received?

• Jesus is really present in the eucharist?

• one receives the body and blood of Christ under the form of bread or wine?

• in some Eastern liturgies, the Eucharistic Prayer takes place behind a screen, hidden from the people?

• Catholics use unleavened bread but most Eastern churches insist on leavened bread for Eucharist?

• the sacrament of penance is also called reconciliation?

• confession of sin is part of the sacrament of penance?

• penance was once reserved for three sins: idolatry, adultery, and murder?

• reconciliation once required years of fasting and penance? (People wishing to be reconciled to the church wore special clothing and begged prayers at the entrance to the church.)

• anointing of the sick used to be called extreme unction?

• any Catholic who is seriously sick may receive anointing of the sick?

• requiring a priest and two other witnesses at a marriage is a rather recent church law?

• under some circumstances the church recognizes common-law marriages?

• divorce was rather commonly practiced in the church for nearly a thousand years?

• Christians were once forbidden to remarry after the death of their spouse?

• holy orders has three grades, unlike any other sacrament?

• the church ordains married men in some countries, and everywhere under special circumstances?

• in the past, young boys were ordained?

• bishops, priests, and deacons all receive the sacrament of holy orders?

Sacramental Symbols

Water: purification

Immersion in water: death to sin

Salt: faith

Oil: strength

Light: Christian life

Rings: unity and endless love

Laying on of hands: transfer of power and healing

Embrace: unity among believers

Bread and wine: signs of Christ's presence

Liturgical Colors

White: purity and joy

Purple/dark blue: sorrow for sin, penitence

Red: courage, love, dedication

Green: hope, peace

Black (no longer used): death

Gold: the fullness of joy

Other Common Symbols

Trumpet: judgment day

Anchor: hope

Acadia bush: immortality

Cedar tree: strength

Evergreen tree: immortality

Fig tree: fruitfulness

Oak tree: strength

Olive tree or branches: peace

Palm branches: joy

Other Symbols

Christian art and liturgy are rich in symbols. Here are a few you will see often:

Symbols of the Trinity

God the Father, Jesus, the Son of God, and the Holy Spirit.

The triangle: Trinity of God

Wheat sheaves: bounty of God

Six-pointed star: God, the Creator

Eye: wisdom and knowledge of God

Dove: Spirit of God

Symbols of Jesus

Lamb: suffering servant of the Lord

Crucifix: death of Jesus

Jeweled cross: the resurrection

Jesus Candle: Christ, the light of the world

Vine and its branches: Jesus, the center of unity among all people

Sun: Jesus, light of the world, source of warmth and power

Crown: Jesus triumphant over death

Heart: Jesus as pure love

Phoenix: Jesus risen from the dead

Pelican: Jesus feeding his children with his own blood

Butterfly: Jesus risen

Alpha and Omega: Jesus the beginning and end of all

INRI: abbreviation for Jesus of Nazareth, King of the Jews

IHS: Greek abbreviation for Jesus, Savior of humankind

Fish: Greek letters stand for Jesus Christ, Son of God, Savior

Chi Rho: Greek abbreviation for Christ

The Four Evangelists

Man sometimes winged: Matthew

Lion: Mark

Ox sometimes winged: Luke

Eagle: John

Church Authority

Bishop's staff or crozier

Tiara or papal crown

Bishop's hat or miter

Keys crossed

Chasuble or outer garment of priests and bishops

Stole (worn over both shoulders of a priest or bishop and over one shoulder of a deacon)

The Order of the Mass

The rites and actions of the Mass are modeled on the family gathering for meals. The family members set the table (the preparation), say grace (the Eucharistic Prayer), and share the food (Communion).

The Introductory Rites (the gathering)

Greeting

Penitential Rite

Kyrie ("Lord, have mercy")

Gloria (in season)

Opening prayer

The Liturgy of the Word

First reading

Responsorial psalm

Second reading

Alleluia

Gospel reading

Homily

Creed

General intercessions

The Liturgy of the Eucharist

Preparation of the gifts

— the presentation of the gifts

— preparation of the bread and wine

Prayer over the gifts

— Preface

— Acclamation (Holy, Holy, Holy)

Eucharistic Prayer

Communion Rite

— the Lord's Prayer

— the breaking of the bread

— Holy Communion

— the prayer after Communion

The Concluding Rite (dismissal)

Greeting

Blessing

Dismissal

About Reconciliation

As Christians we believe that baptism
    brings a person to a whole new life.
We speak of this new life in many different ways,
    for example, being "sinless" and "pleasing to God."
We believe that the newly baptized person
    is as innocent as a newborn baby.
When we Christians slip into a life of sin
    and are cut off from the community of believers,
    we are invited to reform our lives,
    and begin anew to follow Christ.
We do this in the sacrament of penance or reconciliation.
This sacrament includes both the confession of our sins
    and reconciliation with God and community.

During medieval times,
    people sought reconciliation in private from monks,
    and so the custom of private confession was born.
Today we confess our sins to God
    in the presence of a priest
        who represents the community.
He then reconciles us in the community's name.
It is God who forgives sin, of course,
    but it is the community of faith
    that announces that reconciliation in God's name.

The Rite of Penance

After the Second Vatican Council
    the Rite of Penance was changed
    to reflect the communal nature
        of both sin and reconciliation.
This sacrament may be celebrated in different ways.

It may be a one-on-one encounter
   between a penitent and his confessor,
   a group celebration in which each penitent
     confesses his or her sins and receives absolution individually
   or in very special cases the whole group
     may make a general confession of their sin
     and together receive absolution.
The ways we prepare for the sacrament
   and receive it are very similar.
Following is an outline of this rite.

Introduction

Priest and penitent spend a short time focusing on God's loving forgiveness. This is more elaborate for groups than for individuals. For individuals a few words may suffice, while hymns and formal prayers may be necessary to help a group attain the same focus.

Celebration of the Word

One or more readings from the Bible help us remember God's loving kindness. One of these readings is always from the gospels.

Reconciliation

Except in unusual circumstances, each person confesses his or her personal sin, prays for God's forgiveness and then receives a suggested penance from the priest. The priest then repeats the words of absolution, an outward sign that God has indeed forgiven us.

Conclusion

Once again priest and penitent spend a few moments thanking God for his mercy. For groups this will naturally be more elaborate than for individuals.

CHAPTER FIVE

Prayer

Why We Pray

Since medieval times, theologians have identified four reasons why we pray to God. They are:

1. To praise God for his goodness.
2. To thank God for his many gifts to us.
3. To ask God for favors.
4. To ask God for forgiveness.

Ways to Pray

Prayer is essentially a conversation with God.

Prayer exists on different levels, just as our conversations do.

At its most intense level,

    words are unnecessary for prayer.

The three major expressions of prayer

    recognized and encouraged by our tradition are:

    vocal prayer,

    meditation,

    and contemplative prayer.

The Our Father

Our Father, who art in heaven
    hallowed be thy name.
Thy kingdom come;
    thy will be done on earth as it is in heaven.
Give us this day our daily bread;
    and forgive us our trespasses
    as we forgive those who trespass against us;
    and lead us not into temptation,
    but deliver us from evil. Amen.

Hail Mary

Hail, Mary, full of grace,
    the Lord is with you!
Blessed are you among women,
    and blessed is the fruit of your womb, Jesus.
Holy Mary, Mother of God,
    pray for us sinners,
    now and at the hour of our death. Amen.

Doxology

Glory be to the Father
    and to the Son,
    and to the Holy Spirit:
As it was in the beginning, is now,
    and will be forever. Amen.

Jesus Prayer

Lord Jesus Christ,
    Son of the living God,
    have mercy on me, a sinner.

Peace Prayer

Lord, make me an instrument of your peace:
   where there is hatred, let me sow love;
   where there is injury, pardon;
   where there is doubt, faith;
   where there is despair, hope;
   where there is darkness, light;
   and where there is sadness, joy.
O Divine Master, grant that I may not seek so much
   to be consoled as to console,
   to be understood as to understand,
   to be loved as to love.
For it is in giving that we receive,
   it is in pardoning that we are pardoned,
   and it is in dying that we are born to eternal life.

—St. Francis of Assisi

For a Holy Heart

Lord, grant me a holy heart that sees always what is fine and pure
   and is not frightened at the sight of sin,
   but creates order wherever it goes.
Grant me a heart that knows nothing
   of boredom, weeping, and sighing.
Let me not be too concerned
   with the bothersome thing I call myself.
Lord, give me a sense of humor
   and I will find happiness in life
   and profit for others.

—St. Thomas More